*J*u*st*

A

Thought!!

Just A Thought

Copyright Page

Faith + Faith

Written by Nastassia Kinlaw

© [2025] by Nastassia Kinlaw

Published by The Kinlaw's Foundation

In collaboration with Resurrection Press

For more information, visit

The Kinlaw's Foundation: Thekinlawsfoundation@gmail.com

ISBN: 979-8-218-85748-6

Printed in the United States of America

Dedication

I dedicate this book to

my Heavenly Father, my mother, and my earthy dad.

Without them, there is no way on this earth,

I could have begun nor complete this book.

When I began to draft this book,

I had no clear vision of where it would begin or end.

I simply started to write.

As the pages unfold,

you will see how my words and messages.

began to grow and take shape under Gods

guidance.

When I was a young girl,

I used to write and imagine,

I was doing important work.

I wrote songs, designed my clothes,

and dreamed without limits.

But as I got older, rushing to grow up,

I lost my way.

or, I had never truly met

the one He designed me to be.

Until now.

To whoever you are reading this,

I want you to know:

when you start seeking the Father,

He will always bring it right back to you.

Because it is you,

he is reintroducing you to.

While drafting this book,

healing began to manifest.

Old, untouched pain and hidden regret's

rose to the surface.

Yet through every release,

a clearer vision began to form.

and a healed Nastassia was born.

A better version,

a renewed vessel,

hand-crafted by my Father

into the woman I am now.

We are often allowed to become

who the world entices us to be,

who we choose to be.

But God says,

"Now, this is who you are with Me."

Just A Thought

By: Nastassia Kinlaw

Contents

A powerful journey from resistance to redemption, where rebellion becomes a tool for spiritual awakening.

Exploring the connection between human defiance and divine correction.

A poetic revelation of dreams, consciousness, and divine messages through the subconscious mind.

A brief reflection on spiritual clarity, self-respect, and awakening to truth. This piece shows how God reveals what was hidden, helping you understand past relationships, release blame, and step into healing with a renewed sense of self.

Pen to paper of your thought's, and emotions while you read this book.

The Rebellious Spirits

The question that comes to mind is, do we humans have actual superpowers? If we do, the next question would be: how are you using them, for evil or for good? Are there any Superman's soaring in the sky, Black Panthers lurking in the shadows, or Wonder Woman's set to save the day? Or Are there...

Jokers laughing in the dark? Or Thanos tightening his grip on power? Are there Mystiques planning the next big change in evolution's hierarchy? Just how are you using your superhuman power?

As a teenager, I was quite rebellious. I often acted without thinking, I was open, and always wanted my way, no matter what the cost. Let me tell you, it cost a lot more than money could ever buy.

Today, I reflect on those days of enlightenment. I have realized that I also have supernatural powers, and I always have had them. In my days of youth, I was unaware that we humans had them, I thought that those types of things were just for entertainment, you know? for Hollywood purpose's, made for the big screen. As I for most of my teenage year I was wrong.

One of my strongest superhuman powers is "Rebellion." Now please, do not be alarmed; I come in peace. I have learned that this fruit can remain. With the right training and discipline, this can become a strong defense against the scheme of the wicked one. See I have figured out that with Gods wisdom and guidance's; The Spirit of Rebellious can get me out of a lot of situations that it once got me in.

I choose not to rebel against my Creator. Instead, I rebel against my flesh and the one who accuses me before God Day and night.

Those trials and difficult moments in my life were heavy rocks. Even when I came out of the turmoil, the pain of those rocks being thrown remained. Yet, it is written:

"On this rock I will build my church, and the gates of Hades will not overcome it" ***(Matthew 16:18-19)***. *What was meant to harm me, God intended it for good to accomplish what is now being done, the saving of many lives. (Genesis 50:20).*

John 15

Rebellious + Resisted=What?

One of the most respected human traits is our ability to gather information in various ways. The correct term is "Human Senses": hearing, vision, taste, smell, touch, and perception.

Perception is how we process information from our friends. It involves:

- *The hearing ear.*

- *Seeing eye.*

- *The untamed judge of taste.*

- *The tongue's friend, nose! known for sniffing around for information.*

They each have their differences, but they are still the bests of friends known too friendship.

{Matthew 13:16}

God uses this friendship to share important messages with us. He helps us stay aligned with His will. Our lord is gentle and kind, seeking to teach us.

In Matthew 11 verses 28-30, Jesus calls out to us, eagerly welcoming his yoke upon us, Jesus says "For my yoke is easy and my burden is light." Going back to my previous statement.

The body signal resistance to us as stress sensors to our bodies when we go against Gods will. This is where we began to practice, pausing and relining. We all need to seek this way of living and laboring.

The Lord speaks with clarity about a life of luxury. It is better than any earthly promise and more dependable than a 401k plan. He describes a rare and unique peace and joy. I chose the words "rare" and "unique" reflecting on modern views of work, peace, and joy. People seek success, but they often miss the true blessings that God provides.

I come from a real place, where my own choices broke my heart. The quiet pain of the world, often masked by money, family, and friends. This dims our originality. I speak so we can overstand the knowledge that has been handed down to us, the lies...

Stress is not cause by the recurring events of

trivial. Stress is caused because most of us were

not taught God's way of dealing with these,

uncomfortable moment's that we all face. Most of

us were never properly educated on the delicate's

of living a well-structured life, while walking

through the shadows of death.

Let's reflect on the story of Jesus and Lazarus

John 11; once you study this chapter, you will

recognize Jesus attitudes in that tragic moment in

his life. Grieved? Yes, stress? No, verse 41-42. Jesus knew that the Father was living and

overseeing all situations when asked in faith and reasoning of his will.

Our bodies become aware of the outer alignment. When we push back against God's direction. Like "The Prophet Jonah," our bodies feel uneasy. A conflict arises between our spirit and flesh. We recognize that "the spirit is willing, but the flesh is weak." The works of the world offer death; going against God destroys the nervous system.

Jehovah, the God who made heaven and earth, the God of Abraham, Isaac, and Jacob, created us for Himself.

When we oppose His divine plans, it doesn't alter His will. Instead, it disrupts our body's harmony and can cause health issues or even death.

Matthew 13

The Parable of the Sower 13:1-23

The Parable of the Weeds 13:24-30

Rebellious + Resisted= Stress

-Nastassia

Faith + Faith

Enigma

What if the world we live in, the one we see every

day, isn't actually the real world? As I write, I am

thinking about the movie The Matrix. What if,

when we are asleep,

seeing visions, we are actually indulging in the

real realm?

I once spoke with my Irish twin brother about the conscious and subconscious mind. He thinks in our subconscious we are our true selves at the most obedient state of ourselves. I stand in agreement with that statement.

Have you ever had a dream in which someone asked you a question, and you responded? Have you ever asked the Father for a closer relationship or for clarity?

Then, a day or so later, did you dream of

doing something wrong according to God's law?

You may have forgotten that you asked. Sheesh...

In our daily chats and endless social media

scrolling, we often forget what matters.

The meaningful things often get pushed aside until

they fade away.

Many of us think our dreams do not matter, but I challenge you: consider them. This process takes only a moment to hypothesize, assess and conclude.

When has anything happened to your body that meant nothing, or wasn't caused for a reason?

God connects with each person in their own way. This can depend on their faith, personality, what's happening in their lives, or His will.

Dreams are, in truth, enigmas, like putting the pieces of a puzzle together. God is an eminent God. It's intriguing how our subconscious gets the message in a dream. But the challenge arises when our soul tries to share this information with our conscious mind. This is when we work to overstand what was communicated.

Today, 09/12/2025, I dropped my son off at school.

Then, I reflected on a dream that Jehovah had

shared with me. I asked the Lord, "Why don't You

speak to me in a more

straightforward manner?" And I heard the Lord

say, "Then what fun would it be?"

Key Terms:

Understand – *To be in the midst of it. To be beneath knowledge. Being in a position of submission.*

Overstand – *Achieve a higher awareness. This means seeing the deeper truth beyond what appears on the surface.*

Where God Hides the Message

When you have a dream, you are blessed, no matter how wild or unusual it may seem. What I am learning is this: do not get distracted by the odd details, the strange settings, or the scattered

images. Place your attention on the main point of the message, the moving pieces that carry meaning. That is where the truth rests.

A vision met me as I slumbered in my most obedient state. What I saw was a man entangled with me in sheets, our body pressed between the creases of the sheets.

After we were done, he walked into what looked like a restroom. He wrapped a stool in a large sheet of wrapping paper and tucked it beneath a cabinet. (This part of the dream had me festering for a moment)

The setting switch and I saw writing on a computer, like screen. I saw it through my own eyes, and yes, I know it sounds strange but stay with me in this.

It is important to awaken with a still, silent mind. Do not speak right away. Allow your brain space to recall the pattern of the message. Even if you cannot remember the entire dream at first, as you move through your day, your subconscious will reveal the meaning clearly, as long as you do not overcrowd your mind with noise and clutter.

Once my mind started breaking down the symbols, my actions began to speak for themselves.

They guided me, showing me what the instructions were. God still gives warning, preparation, and direction.

He gives tasks and instruction so you can carry out what He places in your spirit. That is exactly why you are reading this page of this book right now.

I will not be lied to; dreams are not just dream,

God did it then and he is still doing it now "he is

the same God, forever."

-Nastassia

Faith + Faith

Fast Talker

Where did this habit of fast talking come from?

Why do some people speak faster than

others? You must discard this habit, and I will

explain why.

Fast talking is not harmless. It's a habit formed in

a world that often told you your

thoughts, opinions, and voice didn't matter. You believed it. You adjusted. And your words began to race.

Often, fast talking is the fruit of abuse. It was born when someone learned to manipulate you, to steal your thoughts and parade them as their own. They cut you off and muted you.

They attacked your character, yet they harbored a hidden desire for your advice. They silenced you in public.

Still, in private, they came knocking, time after time, seeking the wisdom God gave you. And still, they claimed it as their own.

I dare you to ask yourself, why? Why do they cut you down but still seek your reasoning? Why do they mock, yet lean in for your guidance? Meanwhile, you stumble over your words, rushing, gasping to get them out. I'll tell you why.

Because they know the truth. The truth of who you are.

The truth of what you carry. The truth of who you are chosen to be, and it frightens them. They fear the day you hold firm to your fiery baton because then you will be able to stand! no longer kneeling to bandage the cuts of your ankles but kneeling to your source of power.

*In **Matthew 5**, Jesus explained, "we are the light of the world. A town built on a hill cannot be hidden. Neither do people light a lamp and put it under a bowl, instead they put it on its stand, and it gives light to everyone in the house." In the same way, let your light shine before others, so that they may see your good deeds and glorify your Father in heaven.*

So, slow your words. Breathe. You do not have to race. They will wait for you to speak. They trust that your knowledge and guidance are divine. They know you have the wisdom that Jehovah alone has given.

Matthew 7:6 *says Jesus warned: "Do not give dogs what is sacred; do not throw your pearls to pigs. If you do, they may trample* *them under their feet and turn and tear you to pieces."*

Jesus is clear. We do not need to be shaped by wrath or by fear. Our words are treasures. Gold, rubies, and gems. They belong in a treasure box until the time is right. Do not throw them out in fear. Do not rush to hand them over.

We do not force. We do not fight. We wait. We nurture. We honor the gift of speech, the wisdom of God, and we use it with integrity to glorify our Lord Jesus Christ...

Your words are valuable.

*Remember **Colossians 4:5-6:** Be wise in the way you act towards outsiders; make the most of every opportunity. Let your conversation be always full of grace, seasoned with salt, so that you may know how to answer everyone."*

ON THIS PAGE, WRITE YOUR TITLE FOR YOUR FRIST BOOK:

Is it Really Yours?

Read The book of Exodus…....

Have you ever stopped to wonder what happened

to the Promise Land? or

Is it still reachable today?

Many of us are still wandering in the wilderness of

our own minds. We move through life searching

for purpose and

freedom, yet remain trapped by fear, guilt, and

confusion.

The wilderness is not simply a place, but a state of mind. Through a Christ-centered awareness, we can reach the Promise Land by following His ways, seeking divine wisdom, and inviting the Holy Spirit into our lives each day.

I often reflect on the story of Lot and his wife being led out of the city gates of Sodom and Gomorrah with divine instruction not to look back.

Most of us know the story. Lots wife looked back **(Genesis 19:1-29)**. *It is easy to judge her, to ask, "Was she crazy? All she had to do was keep walking."*

As a woman who has experienced my own moments of disobedience, I confess it is not that simple.

For reasons which we do not always understand,

our old ways flare up, tempting us to turn around.

It is in those moments I am reminded of God's

grace, Jesus Christ. Truly, if the Father had not

sent Jesus I too would have turned into salt.

This brings us to a deeper question:

Does anything in this world truly belong to you or

me?

What if our own stories don't belong to us, what if I told you nothing belongs solely to

you nor I, except the choice to honor God and serve others?

What if we can help others reach thee promise land simply by giving what belongs to God? our obedience, our gratitude, our testimony and by giving others what they are due: compassion, truth, and love?

Psychologically, this is where transformation begins. When we surrender the illusion of control and align our thoughts with divine truth, healing begins.

So, how do we reach the Promise Land?

What must we do?

What do we possess that belongs to others?

And how can our journey affect someone else's deliverance?

The truth is nothing in this world belongs to us.

Every trial, every victory, and every moment of

growth must be surrendered to the Father in holy

obedience.

Healing requires honesty about who we are,

where we have been, and who brought us out of

darkness into light.

*In **Matthew 5:13**, it is written:*
"We are the salt of the earth."

Salt preserves, heals, and brings flavor. Likewise, our struggles and victories are meant to be shared to glorify our Heavenly Father and inspire those who follow behind us. Our transparency becomes the bridge between pain and restoration, between lost and found.

Our ancestors were delivered from slavery by the mighty hand of God. He promised them a journey

to a land flowing with milk and honey. Yet, the Israelites wandered for forty years due to disobedience and disbelief. Even after walking through the Red Sea on dry land, they still doubted.

Today, He remains the same God, still delivering, still parting seas, still calling us toward peace and renewal. But many of us are not listening, not obeying, not uniting, and not honoring God by telling the truth of our transformation.

We live in a world where too many minds have become distracted filled not with divine thought, but with noise and empty air.

As Psychology scholar and faith-based wellness writer dedicated to healing through prayer, reflection, and holistic living, I see the wilderness not only as a biblical journey but as a mental and emotional condition.

Healing begins when we shift our mindset from survival to surrender, when we stop wandering and start walking with purpose.

Through faith, honesty, and obedience, the Promise Land is still within reach both in spirit and in the mind.

Strong Holds? Generational Curse? Huh! What is that?

In Jesus Name I Have Been Redeem

This is where you grab your bible and read
Matthew 25:14-30

Sitting With Me, Myself

And

I

Have you ever found yourself sitting with the future you, or the past you? If you are blessed, you get to meet them both. It is an oracle, a divine communication, a revelation. Our old or future selves often find their way back to us in another body, through the different people we meet.

Sometimes it happens in a random conversation, yet the feeling is undeniable, you know this soul.

From the very first words, you feel as if you have known this person all your life. If you are a woman, it feels like you have known her forever; if you are a man, it feels like you have

known him forever.

Laughter fills the air, your imagination stirs, and

the iron wheel of thought begins to spin again.

Tears may fall in between the

laughter, and suddenly your words flow freely.

You find yourself saying, "It feels like I've met you before." Before you realize it, you have shared your entire life story or revealed your deepest secret, and it feels safe,

because it truly is. In that moment, you are speaking to a past you, or future you.

You can tell which one by reflecting on the conversation.

If you are speaking with your past self, you hear yourself say things like,

"I used to do that," or "I did that too." Sometimes those words sting. Something in your mind clicks, and you realize those words could push away someone who mirrors your old wounds. You stop, because you understand, you know the pain of those words.

Coming from such a place, where your past self

sits beside you in the present; it is a call for

wisdom; an intellectual skill that God only

provides: the ability to see the damage

in your own words, to recognize it, and to stop.

Repeating such phrases can make another person

feel small, unseen, or dismissed.

At the same time, those words quietly build pride

in the one speaking them. Blocking the gift of

compassion, with that pride an opportunity is lost,

an opportunity to heal, to release, to smile in the

face of what once

hurt you, and to finally declare within yourself,

"No. It stops right here."

Sitting with your future self

is quite different

When you sit with the person who has walked through the fire, the fire of purification, you begin to recognize your own strength reflected in them. You feel the warmth of their presence and see the light in their eyes.

Their words carry a quiet magical effect on you, and you catch a glimpse of what your future could become.

In this conversation, you find yourself saying things like, "I've been thinking about that," or "I need to do that." A spark of excitement rises within you, and you start taking notes about your next steps. You ask, "How long did it take? Was it hard?"

The mature version of you responds with gentle wisdom. You can feel the love, their smile leading with their smiling eyes, the kind that understands your wounded heart without needing to speak it. Their voice soothes you with unspoken assurance, reminding you softly, "Don't worry, you'll make it."

Between those two moments, there is something resting in the one that feels alive, the one quietly waiting to meet you. Here, clarity does not hide, it greets you with open hands.

Meeting the old you reveal truths about yourself. It shows whether you are healed or still carrying damage.

Ask yourself honestly: did you see your old self in him or her?

Many people never move past this step

because of self-denial. Honesty is what opens the

door to the next question:

how did you treat them?

Did you cry with them in their pain? Did you

nourish them? When you saw

the condition of their heart, did it break your heart

all over again?

Did you speak the words you always wished

someone had spoken to you? or did you exalt

yourself above them?

Did you use words that carried contempt? Did

you truly listen, or did you

rush to speak, when all that was needed was your

silence and presence.

Are you healed?

"A healed person stands in the way of recognizing a damaged soul yet remains the fountain that never becomes the cause or projection of that damage."

-Nastassia

Faith + Faith

Catching My Thought's,

Come here Brain…

Ever reflected on those who once hurt you? those

who tried to belittle you, whether directly or

indirectly?

I can flip a coin and say they probably did it

indirectly.

I find myself recalling those times, and it always

seems to come back at the most unexpected times.

Today, 09/30/2025, I sit here editing my book, reading the words of my Father, and it happened again.

These thoughts came to me:

"I don't have to cheat, lie, steal nor hide

anymore... cause what I have is genuine and he

loves me..."

Those years of the past when you tried to put me

under your foot, attack my character, and gloat in

my season of affliction...

When I cried out just for an ear, only an ear. When I needed you to be there for me without expecting anything in return, because I had nothing to give that wouldn't cost me severely.

During those times, I created a fantasy to shield myself from seeing and believing the truth, just to keep you in my life.

Yet even that wasn't honorable enough for you to love me as I desired, or to give me the same support you once needed from me in return. Instead, you laughed, rolled your eyes, and mentally placed me in the lowest rank of your lives.

For years I kicked, screamed, and cried, asking "why?" while putting on my brightest smile just to come around and still wonder "why?" But now I smile a bigger, brighter smile. When I was asleep, my father gave me instructions. Although I didn't fully comprehend, He kept nudging me to read

"John 15."

The Holy Spirit whispered in my

ear, "Go take a walk." Strangers spoke words of

instruction I had already read, and my soul

already knew. I had to let go.

Then a heavy weight grew. I began to cry out in

torment and pain; it felt as if my flesh was being

torn from my bones. "Oh no," I thought, "I can

see my bones." I cried out as a mother in birth

pain, thinking the word but not daring to say it

aloud to my father.

"Why?"

Days passed, feeling like needles poking my eyes

and back. Some days I wouldn't say a word to

those around me. But one day the light came on,

and baby, it was bright.

*I began to call to mind the book of **Ezekiel37:***

"The hand of the Lord came upon me and brought

me out in the spirit of the Lord and set me down in

the midst of the valley; and it was full of bones.

Then he caused me to pass by them all around, and

behold, there were very many in the open valley

and indeed they were very dry, And he said

to me, "Son of man can these bones live? So, I

answered, "O Lord God, you know. Again, he said

to me, "Prophesy to these bones, and say to them,

O dry bones, hear the word of the Lord! Thus says

the Lord God to these bones: "surely, I will cause

breath to enter you, and you shall live"

These words are the medicine to my healing

powerful and true. They envy me because my

father kept me and always loved me. God has

always had me in His hands, and you all saw it,

saw it before me. It's not that you can't have it too;

the reason you don't is because you are chicken

squash...

I encourage you to put this book down and pick up the bible and continue to read Ezekiel 37 chapter and find your medicine.

Write your Thoughts…

We Have the Product

Roman 6:19

When I was a thief, I moved through stores like a

shadow, taking what I needed to make a profit.

My cousin and I would run it for days at a time.

I remember, as a teenager, telling my mother when

I left the house, "I'll be back, I'm going to work,"

(laughing, smh). That

line became our cover; our lie dressed up as a

hustle.

We were practical about this line of work. Not

glamorous, but efficient. I went to jail a few times

for stealing.

I had to start over each time, losing my home and

my kids' values. My cousin had her own plans.

So, when I jumped, we were ten toes down on any

territory. Hustling the streets, making fast money

for first, last, and security.

Keep in mind, my cousin and I were born and

raised in Dade County, so you can imagine the

amount of money

needed to survive.

When summer ended and Christmas came, we hit

the stores. During the day, we would sneak in and

take what we needed. At night

or on weekends, we sold it.

Thinking back, once we had everything in our

possession,

the feeling was magnificent. Holding it all felt

powerful. There was an electric hush when the

stash was real.

We were a force that no human could stop; we

intended for everything to go. Hell, police officers,

and fear

stood zero chance of stopping us when the product

was in our possession.

We stopped and spoke with everyone. Big, small,

white, Black, Asian, Chinese. Rich, poor. Riding

bikes, walking, driving,

Smoking molly, smoking crack, and rolling dice.

Some people did not buy, but they gave. Someone

once paid my cousin and me to listen while they

told their story. We sat in

rooms with people others dreamed of meeting. We walked through their homes, sat on their couches, and clapped along. If they were cooking, we were eating.

Products passed hand over fist. If you needed something, we could get it. If we didn't want to get it, we would find

someone to do it. We would sell water to a fish. Once our mind was set on a goal, we strategized how to get it done, although strange

but creative methods and it worked.

We would ride down 79th, a street known for

sexual activity and drug use, we weren't looking

for that kind of pleasure. Instead, we asked anyone

if they wanted to make a quick

$200 keeping your legs close and riding in AC. we

would say, "You have to go into two

stores." And they would agree.

We would target the drug users, but sensible ones.

My cousin and I had an eye for the good ones.

Man, we ran into some unique characters. I meant good people, regardless of the circumstances with whom, we shared many laughs. The talks we had on the rides were

amazing. I'll always remember those laughs we shared.

Those nights taught me more about people than any professor or doctor could.

I learned the weight of secrets and what hides under the choice of drugs. I saw myself in them. I saw the tears falling behind the smiling eyes.

Although they smile, I saw the cracks. The dirt under their nails! I knew the reason; they had been digging a hole all night to bury their pain.

Shame and need often swap roles. There's quiet dignity in those who will still tell you the truth if you sit and listen. I heard wisdom spoken from their souls that touched my very own.

We were thieves, yes, but we were witnesses too. We heard confessions in alleys and prayerful pleas in

the drive-thru of McDonald's. We saw hunger in many forms.

The book of Romans says, "For just as you presented your members as slaves of uncleanness, and lawlessness leading to more lawlessness, so now present your members as slaves of righteousness for holiness."

When God gave me understanding of that verse, I cried. When the light began to shine on me, I was quickened to grab my robe, rushing to tie it, yet still feeling shame, for I had

no clothes under my robe.

I was naked before the Lord. My thoughts came

humbly before my Maker, tears shedding from my

eyes. I thought about how far Jehovah has brought

me and the many situations He has dug me out of;

out of the mess I chose to make.

"I shall examine myself."

And what I found was more unworthiness. The audacity of me to ask so much of Him and to show such little gratitude.

He gave me the best job I could ask for: staying home with my husband and kids.

The lord has helped me keep my health and beauty, even with my learning disability. He has inspired me with precious ideas, then he has help

me build the momentum to share my story of

shame, with the Spirit of God guiding it.

My only job is to tell the story, give credit where

it's due to my God, and follow His way to the best

of my ability. For when I fall short of strength,

grow weary, or become confused, I call on Him for

renewal.

I will run with the wind at my back. I won't run aimlessly; I will run with purpose. My goal is to grasp the everlasting crown of eternal life.

I speak to my thieves, or former ones: we indeed have the product, and this, man, let me tell you, weighs far more than gold.

We have the product, and it is good, it is so good. The equality is beyond measure, non-perishable.

The scent of this fragrance could never be bottled.

To taste a flavor such as this is to die for.

We no longer have to bargain for prices.

*it is written, Jesus explains no one can come to him unless the Father has sent **them (John 6:65)**.*

We no longer wait for the afternoon shift to hit the same store we hit in the morning.

We don't have to worry about not getting the product.

We have the merchandise

Lay all shame down at the feet of our Lord. Ask for deliverance, transformation, and watch my Father work. I've got a Master

Worker, and He's so good. The words spoken from

His mouth drips with fiery purification, melting

gold. With His bare hands, He begins to work and

mold, His gaze locked on the creation of the story

He has rewritten.

He is the best author known to man, the painter of

many, many portraits.

He waits, willing and more than able, to write

yours.

Are you looking for a vendor?

I got one.

"Pain is what most of us are running from, so we should also be careful before we judge. Let us examine the man, instead of judging the man"

-Nastassia

Faith + Faith

Regrets

John 15

Healing, inner peace, and manifestation are

popular topics in ads today. It's like healing has

become a trend, sold as if it's going out of style.

But rarely do we hear about the pruning that

comes with the healing process: the parts that

hurt, the parts that get messy.

True healing resembles the early stages of locking your hair. It can be awkward and uncomfortable, and sometimes it's tough to see progress.

Have you ever seen a pruned tree? Now imagine that you are the tree, and the branches are your flesh. Some branches are good, bearing fruit and others are not.

In the pruning process every ugly secret, rotting fruit is being snipped away by the hands of the Gardener.

Living a holistic life, it's vital that we begin to plant, planting tells the story.

By Planting it teaches us the process of transformation. Looking through the lens of a planter we begin to comprehend the stages of healing.

We come to know that we are a part of the healing process, and that it is necessary for us to act in the physical world.

Anything that Jehovah has His hands in is done with perfection in such a way that the human mind cannot fully comprehend or measure.

The type of healing, God does in purity, purer than

a diamond itself. Yet it often involves getting dirty.

those old ugly truths being dug up, opened and

untouched wombs being erupted from the surface

and going through the soil before growth can

manifest

The process of planting a plant:

twice as wide to give it room to grow.

Lift the plant from its container

Loosen the roots that forgot how to breathe.

Set it in the soil so the crown rests level with

the ground, balanced, not buried.

Return the soil, press it gently as if tucking a child

in for rest.

Pour water over the roots until the earth drinks

deeply.

Stand back, watch the soil settle, and know that

something unseen has begun.

Don't forget to water your planted flowers.

Inner work is necessary

Almost everyone I meet wants to be healed

outwardly, but few want to face the inner

work. I get it! I understand. It's painful to confront

the parts of yourself you've hidden

behind the mask of being "okay.," But that is

where true growth begins.

Let me tell you a story.

A young girl and her cousin let's call the cousin Anne. They were close, always had been. Typical cousins, they grew up

competing, teasing, and bonding through the years. As time passed, the rivalry faded, but the bond remained genuine.

.

Later down the line, I allowed outside influences and the spirit of people-pleasing to build a wall between her and I. On a command send from my mother in 2016; I stole money from my cousin. As wrote the word "command" I find myself challenging that word "command" it still feels like disowner ship. Was it really a command? No, it was a choice I made. God gave a precious gift to all humanity, when he gave us the ability to choose, I could have said no, I could have stopped it, but I didn't.

Today, October 16, 2025, I am confronted with that regret but this time, in a different light.

In the beginning, I tried to reason with myself. I blamed the influence, the pressure, the need to please others. But today, I must face the truth: I destroyed our trust by my own choice.

Yes, there were influences. Yes, I was impure in those days. But it was my choice, and nine years later, that choice still meets me where I stand.

Driving down the road today, I said to my Father, "Lord, I am truly sorry I did that to her."

I can say that freely now because I know that is not who I am and never was. I can say I wanted to please my mother, my brother, or that I wanted to fit in and all that might be true but none of it matters now. It was not worth the love we share for each other.

Now I must go through the process of facing myself and understanding how I allowed outside forces to damage the love and safety that once covered us.

An apology alone does not feed her children or pay bills. I have asked my Father to let me repay her. It does not erase what happened, but it restores something deeper: accountability.

God will always dig up old roots that need to be carried back to their rightful owner. There is no such thing as "just forget about it."

When God wants something addressed, He will bring it to the surface.

Maybe my cousin is already healed and has moved on. Maybe there is no void left at all. But understand this there is a deep, divine truth when they say "forgiveness is not for me but for you"

I thank my Father that she is still here

on this earth, because that means I can heal too.

Remember actively heel yourself daily however do

not remain in chains.

Influence, yes! But remember this truth:
It is your choice that is chasing you.

-Nastassia

Faith + Faith

Hidden Regrets? Care to Share? Let Us Create an Action Plan

"Other's indeed have forgiven you, but have you forgiven yourself."

-Nastassia

Faith + Faith

Let's Talk about

Being "Shy"

Let's start challenging some of those phrases that people label as unwanted traits words like shy, territorial, and insecure. The truth behind these emotions reveals a much deeper meaning than most of us were ever taught.

So, let us strip shy of its power and reveal what is really underneath. Let's unmask it together.

Here we go!

The definition of shy is "being reserved or showing nervousness or timidity in the company of others."

The key words here are reserved, nervous, and timid.

And we will close with the phrase, "in the company of others."

Let's start with reserved.

Now, that is a quality we should never lose in our walk with the Lord.

Being reserved allows us to assess potential danger.

In Proverbs 23:1, God tells us when we sit at the table with rulers, we must observe carefully. So, reservedness is wisdom. It is spiritual awareness in motion.

Next comes timidity.

Timidity is defined as "showing a lack of courage or confidence; easily frightened."

Now, this is an interesting one and I will tell you why.

Being timid is actually a valid emotion, but only toward our Heavenly Father.

God did not give us the spirits of fear; however, we are to remain humble amongst one another, Romans 15:1 tells us we who are strong are to

bear with the weakness of those not strong, and not to be pleasing ourselves. We must continually check in with Jesus to make sure we are aligned with God's will.

The other side of timidity; fear, lack of confidence, and anxiety, those emotions will fade once God confirms His word. And trust me, I have experienced this personally.

I have had uncertain times that made me anxious. When God gave me guidance, then more guidance, and lots of confirmation, I realized how personal my relationship with Him really is.

And lately, he has been answering me on time! I thank him for that. That was a personal thought that intruded on me mid-sentence, so I thought I would share it with you.

Now for the third key word nervous.

This one is a signal, like a gentle warning light on your dashboard.

It is not meant to paralyze you it is meant to make you check in.

To me, this feeling acts like the Bat-Signal others

can see it in us, but we must learn to

interpret it. Nervousness often signals God

communicating through our bodies. It prompts us

to pause and evaluate our surroundings.

Ask yourself:

Am I supposed to be here?

Are my words aligned with the Father?

Am I doing something I should not?

Or is there something I am not recognizing?

That is how we mature shyness. We do not reject it, we refine it.

When I meet new people or allow new rulers to sit at my table, it's nerve-racking. And honestly, it should be. That cautiousness keeps me discerning.

I take time to identify and ask myself

who do they serve is it the true living God, or a

false one they've chosen to follow?

No, God did not give us a spirit of fear.

But He did give us wisdom, discernment, and self-

awareness.

To mature this personal trait "shyness" is to understand it and learn how to use it effectively, not let it hinder you.

So, the next time you feel nervous, shy, or timid don't rush to erase it.

Pause. Observe. Pray.

Maybe God is just pruning your branches, preparing you to grow in confidence, and teaching you to stand tall in His presence. This is how we

will mature shyness "in the presence of others."

Philosophy when superficially studied excites

doubt, when thoroughly explored, it dispels it.

-Francis Bacon

Partnership

1. Understanding Relationships

Relationships are important, whether friendship,

family, or marriage. I realize that both involve

strong connections: physical, emotional, and

spiritual. Who we choose to partner, whether it

may be a family member, friend or spouse, is

crucial to our growth.

Yes, your partner may have good traits that serve

you in the here and now. They had lively talks

about all sorts of topics.

They were fun to hang out with and full of passion.

They provided well, listened

closely, and tended to be a "yes-man." The list

goes on.

See you start to uncover your true self, assessing

As you start to uncover your true self, assessing

your circle becomes important. Check if they

reflect your true self and what grounds you.

Remember, your real source of power comes from

the Father.

You must also understand who and what is at work

against your grounding.

2. Spiritual Evaluation:

When you are in a partnership of any sort, you

must pause and ask: Who is the devil using?

Start filtering out the willing vessels, the ones who

do not resist the tricks of the enemy.

Matthew 6:6 Go into a quiet place to pray. Close the door and speak to the Father. Ask Him to reveal your role in the matter and the intentions of those around you.

Often, the very things Satan uses against us are the things or people we have placed above God. It could be our own behavior that' is creating confusions.

The Father might let this happen to show us what holds us back. Regardless, we ask the Father to take care of it. He is skillful in this way.

When the enemy attacks and chaos spreads, we must pause and reflect. In doing so, we may uncover the real problem lies within ourselves.

Even when the enemy attacks and causes chaos,

we can look within. There, we find the real issue.

One thing I have learned about the Father: He will

always bring it back to you. Yes indeed, He will

reveal things about others, but understand, His

deepest concern is you and His relationship with

you.

I speak to you, and to myself, we must remember

everything outside the ring

does not matter. It is He who controls this sea.

Hallelujah, praise the mighty name of Jesus.

3. The Importance of Discernment

When we walk with Jesus, we need not only to watch for the "Judas." We also need to look for the willing vessel.

These are the people who allow the enemy to operate without restrictions.

These individuals can be dangerous to your

spiritual walk.

Some are not willing to change. It is not our job to

do God's job. We are to pray for His moving hand,

not to take over His battles.

Many followers of Christ rush into spiritual battles

meant for God. This often times trap us in the

schemes that Satan has set for us from the very

beginning.

Pause and reflect on Proverbs 5:9. Proverbs 5

warns us of the adulterous spirit, its temptations,

and its behaviors.

4. Choosing a Spiritual Fighter

We must accept the truth: you and I are under

attack daily.

It's not enough to partner with

anyone who simply shows interest in any type of

matter.

We need fighters. People that are given the spirit

to stand and battle beside us. That is the essence of

partnership.

Partnership: *An association of two or more people*

joined for a shared purpose.

When we join with another on an intimate level, we

must discern their intentions and spirit.

Liberating vessels of any type of evil force is

damaging not only to our growth but also to our

health. The attack of the evil one throws

us off track; it is a setback. That kind of blow,

thrown by a dark force, feels different.

It provokes emotional responses that do not come

from wisdom or humility.

Satan has nothing to do but cause delays. But we

will not allow the delay to be permit,

for we seek a full life here on planet Earth. If we

don't notice this and ask for help, we

might end up lost in the desert, our bones left to rot

in the wilderness.

Let us put this into practice:

Before shaking hands, signing contracts, and

touching and agreeing.

Let us assess the

individuals. Let's see what the Lord says about

their power level. He is the best advisor and

mentor I know.

1 Samuel 16:7 He judges not by appearance but by

the heart.

Please, put this book down and grab the Bible,

Continue reading (1 Samuel 16)

Prayer of Discernment and

Protection

Father, you are our grand creator. You are the one

who paves the rocky road smooth for us to walk on

leveled ground. You are the author of every living

and non-living thing. It is you who produces

knowledge so man can shoot forth. You are the

provider of all

things. You call to pass things that were not into

existence.

Forgive my unclean ways, shame, and doubt.

Father, you said that we must speak to the

mountain in a direct manner, and it will be cast

into the sea.

I have placed the spirit of discouragement, bad

associations, and negativity at my holy

Father's feet. I command you to leave my presence

by the power of my Father, in Jesus' name. You

will depart from among me. According to the

blood of Jesus, you will be condemned because

you have chosen to rise against me. According to

Christ Jesus, I am not afraid of you because I can

do all things in my Father who strengthens me.

My Lord Jesus has seen you and your followers

falling from heaven, so now you have no powers.

In John 10:28, my Father promises us everlasting

life. We will never be destroyed, and no one can

take us from His hands.

What you will do, is wait for your banishment in

the name of my Lord and Savior, Jesus Christ.

Amen.

Who knows the thought of a man?

Jehovah and the man alone.

A Call for

Renewal, Balance's & Healing

Father, forgive us for our foolish engagement with

unknown spirits. We signed unholy contracts that

go against You alone.

Our father in heaven, I enter your house of prayer

with a humble heart in Jesus Name:

Father, pour out your discernment on your sons

and daughters like the waters of the sea. Help us

notice when we are near your

angels, prophets, and atoning servants. Let the

scales fall from our eyes. Restore our sight. Give

us the speech and languages of your holy divine

truth.

Father, please lift dementia. Let your people

remember and share your great works with their

children and grandchildren. Father, heal the

paralyzed; mentally, physically, and

spiritually. Father, bless the feet of your disciples and give strong, truthful testimony of your still-moving hand.

Father, rise up in your anger, pour out your wrath against HIV, Cancer, Hepatitis, and all unclean spirits hidden in sickness, designed to cause your people to lose hope in you. Send forth your servant with the power of true healing, Father. Strengthen your angels and prepare them for the coming out, Lord.

Let your rain heal the ground; let it produce your fine herbs, fruits, and vegetables. Stop the slaughter of your beautiful creation made by your majestic hands, holy and true you are.

We, as your followers, children, and bond servants, wait in expectation. Father, may our eyes see it.

Only if you agree with this prayer, please say Amen in Jesus' Name.

Reflection

As a psychology student and a person of faith, I know partnership is both emotional and spiritual. Healthy relationships require discernment, prayer, and self-awareness. The right partnership strengthens your mind and spirit. The wrong one drains both. Let this prayer guides you in choosing relationships that show God's order, where peace and purpose come together.

Turn on the Light's

I understand now what I did,

how I ruined relationships by letting myself be

ruled.

How I gave permission quietly, unknowingly

to be attacked.

I wasn't respecting myself,

so how could I expect respect from any of you?

Yes, I gave respect,

and demanded it back without ever standing up for

myself.

My voice bent,

my truth dodged,

and I stepped aside from the very love

I always had a fair chance of receiving from the

beginning.

And I also know now

what you did to me had nothing to do with me.

Yes, I placed myself in your path and felt the

affliction,

but the affliction wasn't mine to carry.

It wasn't a sign about me.

I closed my eyes to what the world really was.

I asked the Father to let me see people, places, and

things

as they truly are, not as they appear.

And what I saw was the same spirit we all share

a craving to love,

to be right,

to be appreciated,

and mostly to be seen

under the weight of this unfair world.

A world where we didn't receive the fruit,

only the stones thrown at us.

So I prayed for Jesus to save us all.

The journey within the soul

mixed with pain, anger, and passion has

created a storm.

It births an uncanny, unrecognizable version of

you and me,

where we stop operating like thinking humans

and become clay,

rolled, reshaped,

smashed into whatever form life decides.

But now I understand:

loving someone properly means loving yourself

first.

And that is the hardest work of all.

To show up for someone else,

you must know how to show up for yourself

in spirit and in truth.

So yes, I apologize

for expecting you to stand for me

without checking if you were even standing for

yourself.

That is what self-love really is.

I should have shown up for me as well.

So no

this is not goodbye.

And no......

this is not me building a wall between you and me.

That is not what you see.

What you see...

are waves.

Waves of me showing up for myself,

and this kind of showing up is exclusive.

Dedicated.

Intentional.

For the first time done properly.

While I am in this waiting room of becoming,

I pray that you too are showing up for you.

So when we meet again,

we meet healed, whole,

and able to experience the wildest

and most breathtaking reunion ever.

From me to You

See, I never tried to put you down or say things

that made you feel empty, less valued, that was

never my intention.

Those words I used were the only ones I had left,

the ones I thought would save you.

See, I was losing... and I was afraid.

I pulled knives, weapons of all sorts, casting down curses, unaware that all I was doing was pushing you away.

I wish I had listened when you said I was taking you for granted.

I wish I had acted when we walked those streets, looking for a Dad, someone to not

Tell you, but show you why the river flows, how the

sun can rise and still cool the cold.

That, my love, was Love.

I watched you closely in your search for

friendship.

Even as an adult, envy still followed you,

I saw you, still accepting roses without their

thorns.

I should have said something, but I kept my mouth

closed.

How could you ever forgive me?

Still, I apologize.

I judged you.

And look! I was right there when you started

wearing costumes, attending masquerades,

indulging in all types of deadly spices.

Man, I should have told you then.

I should have listened.

When you sat among your peers, knowing deep

down that you and them were not the

same, not in spirit, not in heart.

I couldn't understand.

So, I judged you again.

And then I checked out on you.

I thought "better you then me,"

but I didn't realize… I am you.

Because we are one.

I left you there.

And you remained seated, waving your hand in the

air, crying out, "Pick me."

I would watch from afar, tears raging in my eyes,

knowing deep inside… no, baby, you were never

picked.

I should have told you then.

I should have fought for you.

But I coward away.

One day, I embraced you in those days of

unexplainable pain, when you cried.

And as I spoke, like I always did in those times,

a voice responded back to me and you.

And the voice said, "I have been with you since

you were little girl.

We quivered in tears of relieve together."

Roses come with thorns, my love.

Man has cultivated this fictional idea of

love, love without pain.

But love without pain has no root, no endurance,

nor character

it shapes nothing.

So they lied and smiled,

stood under their fixture lights,

claiming love cost nothing,

while slowly betting you in,

twisting the knife in your back

as you held the rose, inhaling poison in vows you

thought were holy.

To those wandering the streets, looking for a

father's love, longing to be picked,

I must tell you; all of this was by design.

You were never meant to be "picked."

Because, baby, you were already chosen.

Spirit to spirit, the light Christ placed in you has

always been known,

that's why they despised.

Mistakes? Regrets? Yes, many.

But you were and are designed for good, not evil.

So today, now that we are aligned, you and me, we

shake hands, raising them to our Heavenly Father,

humble and thankful,

inviting the Holy Spirit daily into our lives,

waiting and expecting His perfect will to be done

in our lives, In Jesus Name

Go in Peace……

SEEK GODS NAME AS FOR HIDDEN TREASURE, TURN TO THE NEXT PAGE

Write the meaning

1. Jehovah:

2. Jehovah Jirah:

3. Jehovah Nissi:

4. Jehovah Shammah:

5. Jehovah Tsidkenu:

6. Jehovah Sabaoth:

7. Jehovah Elohim:

8. YHWH:

8. *Jehovah Rapha:*

9. *El Shaddai:*

10. *Adonai*

Closing Prayer For you

Father this is what I ask of you; that you bless the reader, give them a heart of discernment, let them hear you voice, give them also a heart quicken to your voice, father may they know your name and receive Jesus Christ as their lord and savior.

Father, I ask you this in Jesus' name.

Testimony, Comments, followship are welcomed

on my social media.

f   *Resurrection Press*

📷 *Press Resurrection*

Closing Thought…….

www.ingramcontent.com/pod-product-compliance
Lightning Source LLC
Chambersburg PA
CBHW030828090426
42737CB00009B/921